The Miss Medal

by Chris Parker
Illustrated by Emma Levey

In this story ...

Pip and Kit help people get their lost things back.

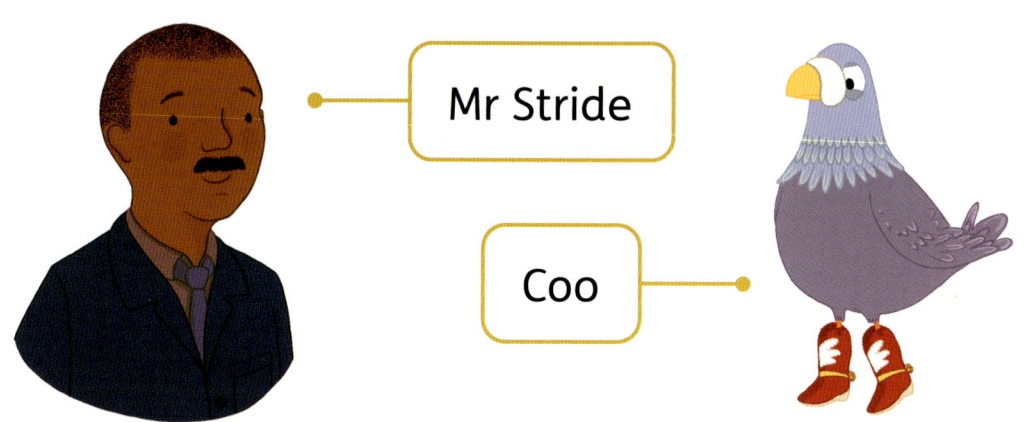

"Ready ... steady ... GO!"
Mr Stride, the race organizer, sounded the horn.
The runners sped off from the starting line.

Pip and Kit clapped as the runners dashed by.
"Next time there's a race, I want to run in it," Pip said.
"Me too," said Kit. "We should start training!"

Suddenly, Mr Stride shouted, "Oh no!"
"What do you think is the matter?" Pip said to Kit.
Kit shrugged.

Pip was <u>curious</u> to know what Mr Stride was shouting about. She wanted to know more. Are you <u>curious</u> too?

"The winner's medal is missing!" Mr Stride said. He was holding an empty box. "We must get it back urgently. The race will end soon!"
"This sounds like a job for us!" Pip said.

Just then, there was a crunching noise. It sounded like footsteps on dry leaves. Pip spotted a bird in a red cap and top running away.

Pip saw a flash of gold. "It's the medal!" she said. "Stop, thief!"
The thief's cap fell off.
"Hey! It's Coo!" cried Kit. "After him!"

"You will have to run faster than that, my friends!" Coo said merrily.

Suddenly, Mr Stride stepped in front of Pip and Kit, blocking their way.

"The race is nearly over!" Mr Stride said. "What are we going to give the winner?"

"We have lost Coo!" Kit said.

"Hang on," whispered Pip. "I think he's <u>beneath</u> that bush!"

Pip has spotted Coo <u>beneath</u> the bush. Can you see anything near you that is <u>beneath</u> something else?

Pip and Kit raced to the bush, but Coo had disappeared.
"<u>Remind</u> me to tell Coo off when we find him," Kit grumbled.

What might Pip say to Kit to <u>remind</u> him to tell Coo off?

Just then, Pip spotted Coo hiding behind a tree trunk. "Over there!" she said.
"I will go around the left side of the tree," Kit said. "You take the right side."

Pip and Kit were out of luck.
Kit let out a groan. "Coo has vanished again," he said.

"No, wait," Pip said, turning round. "He's by those trucks!"

They began to sneak up on Coo.

"Shh!" Kit said. "Don't let him hear us."

Pip has <u>discovered</u> Coo's hiding place. Have you ever played a game where you had to <u>discover</u> where someone was hiding?

Pip and Kit could hear Coo speaking to himself. "This medal looks very good on me," he said. "I think I will keep it on all the time!"

Suddenly ... *SNAP!* Kit stepped on a twig. Pip gasped. Coo turned quickly.

Coo instantly started running. "Did you think you could creep up on me?" he shouted. "You were stomping around like elephants!"

Another word for 'instantly' is <u>immediately</u>. Can you think of something else Coo could <u>immediately</u> start doing when he sees Pip and Kit?

Pip and Kit chased after Coo again. Coo flapped his wings and tried to take off. The medal was too heavy. It was hard for him to fly.

Kit did a huge leap into the air. He grabbed the medal from around Coo's neck.

Coo flew down and tried to yank the medal back off Kit. Coo gave it a hard jerk.
The medal shot out of Kit's paws and sailed over the race track.

The winner was just crossing the finish line.
The medal landed around her neck.
The crowd went wild!

The winner <u>received</u> her medal in a very surprising way. How would you usually <u>receive</u> a medal?

"Good job, Kit!" Pip said. "Next time, we will both run in the race."

"I am not sure about that now ... my paws ache," said Kit. "I think I will go by bicycle!"

Retell the story